Defoe
Abbott
Marx
Hardy
Montaigne
Machiavelli
Haggard
Chesterton
Cooper
Emerson
Joyce
Austen
Hugo
Eliot
Grimm
Melville
Stoker
Carroll
Christie
Maupassant
Byron
Molière
Schiller
Wilde
Garnett
Fitzgerald
Einstein
Hawthorne
Engels
Smith
Kafka
Hall
Goethe
Dostoyevsky
Cotton
Kipling
Doyle
Willis
Baum
Henry
Nietzsche
Leslie
Dumas
Flaubert
Turgenev
Balzac
Stockton
Vatsyayana
Crane
Burroughs
Verne
Curtis
Tocqueville
Whitman
Gogol
Vinci
Homer
Widger
Tolstoy
Busch
Darwin
Thoreau
Twain
Potter
Freud
Zola
Lawrence
Scott
Plato
Harte
Kant
Jowett
Stevenson
Dickens
Andersen
London
Descartes
Cervantes
Burton
Hesse
Poe
Aristotle
Wells
Voltaire
Cooke
Hale
James
Hastings
Bunner
Shakespeare
Irving
Richter
Chambers
Chekhov
Benedict
Alcott
Doré
da Shaw
Wodehouse
Pushkin
Dante
Swift
Newton

 tredition®

tredition was established in 2006 by Sandra Latusseck and Soenke Schulz. Based in Hamburg, Germany, tredition offers publishing solutions to authors and publishing houses, combined with world-wide distribution of printed and digital book content. tredition is uniquely positioned to enable authors and publishing houses to create books on their own terms and without conventional manu-facturing risks.

For more information please visit: www.tredition.com

TREDITION CLASSICS

This book is part of the TREDITION CLASSICS series. The creators of this series are united by passion for literature and driven by the intention of making all public domain books available in printed format again - worldwide. Most TREDITION CLASSICS titles have been out of print and off the bookstore shelves for decades. At tredi-tion we believe that a great book never goes out of style and that its value is eternal. Several mostly non-profit literature projects pro-vide content to tredition. To support their good work, tredition donates a portion of the proceeds from each sold copy. As a reader of a TREDITION CLASSICS book, you support our mission to save many of the amazing works of world literature from oblivion. See all available books at www.tredition.com.

Project Gutenberg

The content for this book has been graciously provided by Project Gutenberg. Project Gutenberg is a non-profit organization founded by Michael Hart in 1971 at the University of Illinois. The mission of Project Gutenberg is simple: To encourage the creation and distribu-tion of eBooks. Project Gutenberg is the first and largest collection of public domain eBooks.

The Thirty Years War —Volume 04

Friedrich Schiller

Imprint

This book is part of TREDITION CLASSICS

Author: Friedrich Schiller
Cover design: Buchgut, Berlin – Germany

Publisher: tredition GmbH, Hamburg - Germany
ISBN: 978-3-8424-6441-4

www.tredition.com
www.tredition.de

HISTORY OF THE THIRTY YEARS' WAR IN GERMANY.

BOOK IV.

The weak bond of union, by which Gustavus Adolphus contrived to hold together the Protestant members of the empire, was dissolved by his death: the allies were now again at liberty, and their alliance, to last, must be formed anew. By the former event, if unremedied, they would lose all the advantages they had gained at the cost of so much bloodshed, and expose themselves to the inevitable danger of becoming one after the other the prey of an enemy, whom, by their union alone, they had been able to oppose and to master. Neither Sweden, nor any of the states of the empire, was singly a match with the Emperor and the League; and, by seeking a peace under the present state of things, they would necessarily be obliged to receive laws from the enemy. Union was, therefore, equally indispensable, either for concluding a peace or continuing the war. But a peace, sought under the present circumstances, could not fail to be disadvantageous to the allied powers. With the death of Gustavus Adolphus, the enemy had formed new hopes; and however gloomy might be the situation of his affairs after the battle of Lutzen, still the death of his dreaded rival was an event too disastrous to the allies, and too favourable for the Emperor, not to justify him in entertaining the most brilliant expectations, and not to encourage him to the prosecution of the war. Its inevitable consequence, for the moment at least, must be want of union among the allies, and what might not the Emperor and the League gain from such a division of their enemies? He was not likely to sacrifice such prospects, as the present turn of affairs held out to him, for any peace, not highly beneficial to himself; and such a peace the allies would not be disposed to accept. They naturally determined, therefore, to continue the war, and for this purpose, the maintenance of the existing union was acknowledged to be indispensable.

But how was this union to be renewed? and whence were to be derived the necessary means for continuing the war? It was not the power of Sweden, but the talents and personal influence of its late king, which had given him so overwhelming an influence in Germany, so great a command over the minds of men; and even he had innumerable difficulties to overcome, before he could establish among the states even a weak and wavering alliance. With his death vanished all, which his personal qualities alone had rendered practicable; and the mutual obligation of the states seemed to cease with the hopes on which it had been founded. Several impatiently threw off the yoke which had always been irksome; others hastened to seize the helm which they had unwillingly seen in the hands of Gustavus, but which, during his lifetime, they did not dare to dispute with him. Some were tempted, by the seductive promises of the Emperor, to abandon the alliance; others, oppressed by the heavy burdens of a fourteen years' war, longed for the repose of peace, upon any conditions, however ruinous. The generals of the army, partly German princes, acknowledged no common head, and no one would stoop to receive orders from another. Unanimity vanished alike from the cabinet and the field, and their common weal was threatened with ruin, by the spirit of disunion.

Gustavus had left no male heir to the crown of Sweden: his daughter Christina, then six years old, was the natural heir. The unavoidable weakness of a regency, suited ill with that energy and resolution, which Sweden would be called upon to display in this trying conjuncture. The wide reaching mind of Gustavus Adolphus had raised this unimportant, and hitherto unknown kingdom, to a rank among the powers of Europe, which it could not retain without the fortune and genius of its author, and from which it could not recede, without a humiliating confession of weakness. Though the German war had been conducted chiefly on the resources of Germany, yet even the small contribution of men and money, which Sweden furnished, had sufficed to exhaust the finances of that poor kingdom, and the peasantry groaned beneath the imposts necessarily laid upon them. The plunder gained in Germany enriched only a few individuals, among the nobles and the soldiers, while Sweden itself remained poor as before. For a time, it is true, the national glory reconciled the subject to these burdens, and the sums exacted, seemed but as a loan placed at interest, in the fortunate hand of Gustavus Adolphus, to be richly repaid by the grateful monarch at the conclusion of a glorious peace. But with the king's death this hope vanished, and the deluded people now loudly demanded relief from their burdens.

But the spirit of Gustavus Adolphus still lived in the men to whom he had confided the administration of the kingdom. However dreadful to them, and unexpected, was the intelligence of his death, it did not deprive them of their manly courage; and the spirit of ancient Rome, under the invasion of Brennus and Hannibal, animated this noble assembly. The greater the price, at which these hard-gained advantages had been purchased, the less readily could they reconcile themselves to renounce them: not unrevenged was a king to be sacrificed. Called on to choose between a doubtful and exhausting war, and a profitable but disgraceful peace, the Swedish council of state boldly espoused the side of danger and honour; and with agreeable surprise, men beheld this venerable senate acting with all the energy and enthusiasm of youth. Surrounded with watchful enemies, both within and without, and threatened on every side with danger, they armed themselves against them all, with equal prudence and heroism, and laboured to extend their kingdom, even at the moment when they had to struggle for its existence.

The decease of the king, and the minority of his daughter Christina, renewed the claims of Poland to the Swedish throne; and King Ladislaus, the son of Sigismund, spared no intrigues to gain a party in Sweden. On this ground, the regency lost no time in proclaiming the young queen, and arranging the administration of the regency. All the officers of the kingdom were summoned to do homage to their new princess; all correspondence with Poland prohibited, and the edicts of previous monarchs against the heirs of Sigismund, confirmed by a solemn act of the nation. The alliance with the Czar of Muscovy was carefully renewed, in order, by the arms of this prince, to keep the hostile Poles in check. The death of Gustavus

Adolphus had put an end to the jealousy of Denmark, and removed the grounds of alarm which had stood in the way of a good understanding between the two states. The representations by which the enemy sought to stir up Christian IV. against Sweden were no longer listened to; and the strong wish the Danish monarch entertained for the marriage of his son Ulrick with the young princess, combined, with the dictates of a sounder policy, to incline him to a neutrality. At the same time, England, Holland, and France came forward with the gratifying assurances to the regency of continued friendship and support, and encouraged them, with one voice, to prosecute with activity the war, which hitherto had been conducted with so much glory. Whatever reason France might have to congratulate itself on the death of the Swedish conqueror, it was as fully sensible of the expediency of maintaining the alliance with Sweden. Without exposing itself to great danger, it could not allow the power of Sweden to sink in Germany. Want of resources of its own, would either drive Sweden to conclude a hasty and disadvantageous peace with Austria, and then all the past efforts to lower the ascendancy of this dangerous power would be thrown away; or necessity and despair would drive the armies to extort from the Roman Catholic states the means of support, and France would then be regarded as the betrayer of those very states, who had placed themselves under her powerful protection. The death of Gustavus, far from breaking up the alliance between France and Sweden, had only rendered it more necessary for both, and more profitable for France. Now, for the first time, since he was dead who had stretched his protecting arm over Germany, and guarded its frontiers against the encroaching designs of France, could the latter safely pursue its designs upon Alsace, and thus be enabled to sell its aid to the German Protestants at a dearer rate.

Strengthened by these alliances, secured in its interior, and defended from without by strong frontier garrisons and fleets, the regency did not delay an instant to continue a war, by which Sweden had little of its own to lose, while, if success attended its arms, one or more of the German provinces might be won, either as a conquest, or indemnification of its expenses. Secure amidst its seas, Sweden, even if driven out of Germany, would scarcely be exposed to greater peril, than if it voluntarily retired from the contest, while the former measure was as honourable, as the latter was disgraceful. The more boldness the regency displayed, the more confidence would they inspire among their confederates, the more respect among their enemies, and the more favourable conditions might they anticipate in the event of peace. If they found themselves too weak to execute the wide-ranging projects of Gustavus, they at least owed it to this lofty model to do their utmost, and to yield to no difficulty short of absolute necessity. Alas, that motives of self-interest had too great a share in this noble determination, to demand our unqualified admiration! For those who had nothing themselves to suffer from the calamities of war, but were rather to be enriched by it, it was an easy matter to resolve upon its continuation; for the German empire was, in the end, to defray the expenses; and the provinces on which they reckoned, would be cheaply purchased with the few troops they sacrificed to them, and with the generals who were placed at the head of armies, composed for the most part of Germans, and with the honourable superintendence of all the operations, both military and political.

But this superintendence was irreconcileable with the distance of the Swedish regency from the scene of action, and with the slowness which necessarily accompanies all the movements of a council.

To one comprehensive mind must be intrusted the management of Swedish interests in Germany, and with full powers to determine at discretion all questions of war and peace, the necessary alliances, or the acquisitions made. With dictatorial power, and with the whole influence of the crown which he was to represent, must this important magistrate be invested, in order to maintain its dignity, to enforce united and combined operations, to give effect to his orders, and to supply the place of the monarch whom he succeeded. Such a man was found in the Chancellor Oxenstiern, the first minister, and what is more, the friend of the deceased king, who, acquainted with all the secrets of his master, versed in the politics of Germany, and in the relations of all the states of Europe, was unquestionably the fittest instrument to carry out the plans of Gustavus Adolphus in their full extent.

Oxenstiern was on his way to Upper Germany, in order to assemble the four Upper Circles, when the news of the king's death reached him at Hanau. This was a heavy blow, both to the friend and the statesman. Sweden, indeed, had lost but a king, Germany a protector; but Oxenstiern, the author of his fortunes, the friend of his soul, and the object of his admiration. Though the greatest sufferer in the general loss, he was the first who by his energy rose from the blow, and the only one qualified to repair it. His penetrating glance foresaw all the obstacles which would oppose the execution of his plans, the discouragement of the estates, the intrigues of hostile courts, the breaking up of the confederacy, the jealousy of the leaders, and the dislike of princes of the empire to submit to foreign authority. But even this deep insight into the existing state of things, which revealed the whole extent of the evil, showed him also the means by which it might be overcome. It was essential to revive the drooping courage of the weaker states, to meet the secret machinations of the enemy, to allay the jealousy of the more powerful allies, to rouse the friendly powers, and France in particular, to active assistance; but above all, to repair the ruined edifice of the German alliance, and to reunite the scattered strength of the party by a close and permanent bond of union. The dismay which the loss of their leader occasioned the German Protestants, might as readily dispose them to a closer alliance with Sweden, as to a hasty peace with the Emperor; and it depended entirely upon the course pursued, which of these alternatives they would adopt. Every thing might be lost by the slightest sign of despondency; nothing, but the confidence which Sweden showed in herself, could kindle among the Germans a noble feeling of self-confidence. All the attempts of Austria, to detach these princes from the Swedish alliance, would be unavailing, the moment their eyes became opened to their true interests, and they were instigated to a public and formal breach with the Emperor.

Before these measures could be taken, and the necessary points settled between the regency and their minister, a precious opportunity of action would, it is true, be lost to the Swedish army, of which the enemy would be sure to take the utmost advantage. It was, in short, in the power of the Emperor totally to ruin the Swedish interest in Germany, and to this he was actually invited by the prudent councils of the Duke of Friedland. Wallenstein advised him to proclaim a universal amnesty, and to meet the Protestant states with favourable conditions. In the first consternation produced by the fall of Gustavus Adolphus, such a declaration would have had the most powerful effects, and probably would have brought the wavering states back to their allegiance. But blinded by this unexpected turn of fortune, and infatuated by Spanish counsels, he anticipated a more brilliant issue from war, and, instead of listening to these propositions of an accommodation, he hastened to augment his forces. Spain, enriched by the grant of the tenth of the ecclesiastical possessions, which the pope confirmed, sent him considerable supplies, negociated for him at the Saxon court, and hastily levied troops for him in Italy to be employed in Germany. The Elector of Bavaria also considerably increased his military force; and the restless disposition of the Duke of Lorraine did not permit him to remain inactive in this favourable change of fortune. But while the enemy were thus busy to profit by the disaster of Sweden, Oxenstiern was diligent to avert its most fatal consequences.

Less apprehensive of open enemies, than of the jealousy of the friendly powers, he left Upper Germany, which he had secured by conquests and alliances, and set out in person to prevent a total defection of the Lower German states, or, what would have been almost equally ruinous to Sweden, a private alliance among themselves. Offended at the boldness with which the chancellor assumed the direction of affairs, and inwardly exasperated at the thought of being dictated to by a Swedish nobleman, the Elector of Saxony again meditated a dangerous separation from Sweden; and the only question in his mind was, whether he should make full terms with the Emperor, or place himself at the head of the Protestants and form a third party in Germany. Similar ideas were cherished by Duke Ulric of Brunswick, who, indeed, showed them openly enough by forbidding the Swedes from recruiting within his dominions, and inviting the Lower Saxon states to Luneburg, for the purpose of forming a confederacy among themselves. The Elector of Brandenburg, jealous of the influence which Saxony was likely to attain in Lower Germany, alone manifested any zeal for the interests of the Swedish throne, which, in thought, he already destined for his son. At the court of Saxony, Oxenstiern was no doubt honourably received; but, notwithstanding the personal efforts of the Elector of Brandenburg, empty promises of continued friendship were all which he could obtain. With the Duke of Brunswick he was more successful, for with him he ventured to assume a bolder tone. Sweden was at the time in possession of the See of Magdeburg, the bishop of which had the power of assembling the Lower Saxon circle. The chancellor now asserted the rights of the crown, and by this spirited proceeding, put a stop for the present to this dangerous assembly designed by the duke. The main object, however, of his present journey and of his future endeavours, a general confederacy of the Protestants, miscarried entirely, and he was obliged to content himself with some unsteady alliances in the Saxon circles, and with the weaker assistance of Upper Germany.

As the Bavarians were too powerful on the Danube, the assembly of the four Upper Circles, which should have been held at Ulm, was removed to Heilbronn, where deputies of more than twelve cities of the empire, with a brilliant crowd of doctors, counts, and princes, attended. The ambassadors of foreign powers likewise, France, England, and Holland, attended this Congress, at which Oxenstiern appeared in person, with all the splendour of the crown whose representative he was. He himself opened the proceedings, and conducted the deliberations. After receiving from all the assembled estates assurances of unshaken fidelity, perseverance, and unity, he required of them solemnly and formally to declare the Emperor and the league as enemies. But desirable as it was for Sweden to exasperate the ill-feeling between the emperor and the estates into a formal rupture, the latter, on the other hand, were equally indisposed to shut out the possibility of reconciliation, by so decided a step, and to place themselves entirely in the hands of the Swedes. They maintained, that any formal declaration of war was useless and superfluous, where the act would speak for itself, and their firmness on this point silenced at last the chancellor. Warmer disputes arose on the third and principal article of the treaty, concerning the means of prosecuting the war, and the quota which the several states ought to furnish for the support of the army. Oxenstiern's maxim, to throw as much as possible of the common burden on the states, did not suit very well with their determination to give as little as possible. The Swedish chancellor now experienced, what had been felt by thirty emperors before him, to their cost, that of all difficult undertakings, the most difficult was to extort money from the Germans. Instead of granting the necessary sums for the new armies to be raised, they eloquently dwelt upon the calamities occasioned by the former, and demanded relief from the old burdens, when they were required to submit to new. The irritation which the chancellor's demand for money raised among the states, gave rise to a thousand complaints; and the outrages committed by the troops, in their marches and quarters, were dwelt upon with a startling minuteness and truth.

In the service of two absolute monarchs, Oxenstiern had but little opportunity to become accustomed to the formalities and cautious proceedings of republican deliberations, or to bear opposition with patience. Ready to act, the instant the necessity of action was apparent, and inflexible in his resolution, when he had once taken it, he was at a loss to comprehend the inconsistency of most men, who, while they desire the end, are yet averse to the means. Prompt and impetuous by nature, he was so on this occasion from principle; for every thing depended on concealing the weakness of Sweden, under a firm and confident speech, and by assuming the tone of a lawgiver, really to become so. It was nothing wonderful, therefore, if, amidst these interminable discussions with German doctors and deputies, he was entirely out of his sphere, and if the deliberateness which distinguishes the character of the Germans in their public deliberations, had driven him almost to despair. Without respecting a custom, to which even the most powerful of the emperors had been obliged to conform, he rejected all written deliberations which suited so well with the national slowness of resolve. He could not conceive how ten days could be spent in debating a measure, which with himself was decided upon its bare suggestion. Harshly, however, as he treated the States, he found them ready enough to assent to his fourth motion, which concerned himself. When he pointed out the necessity of giving a head and a director to the new confederation, that honour was unanimously assigned to Sweden, and he himself was humbly requested to give to the common cause the benefit of his enlightened experience, and to take upon himself the burden of the supreme command. But in order to prevent his abusing the great powers thus conferred upon him, it was proposed, not without French influence, to appoint a number of overseers, in fact, under the name of assistants, to control the expenditure of the common treasure, and to consult with him as to the levies, marches, and quarterings of the troops. Oxenstiern long and strenuously resisted this limitation of his authority, which could not fail to trammel him in the execution of every enterprise requiring promptitude or secrecy, and at last succeeded, with difficulty, in obtaining so far a modification of it, that his management in affairs of war was to be uncontrolled. The chancellor finally approached the delicate point of the indemnification which Sweden was to expect at the conclusion of the war, from the gratitude of the allies, and flattered himself with the hope that Pomerania, the main object of Sweden, would be assigned to her, and that he would obtain from the provinces, assurances of effectual cooperation in its acquisition. But he could obtain nothing more than a vague assurance, that in a general peace the interests of all parties would be attended to. That on this point, the caution of the estates was not owing to any regard for the constitution of the empire, became manifest from the liberality they evinced towards the chancellor, at the expense of the most sacred laws of the empire. They were ready to grant him the archbishopric of Mentz, (which he already held as a conquest,) and only with difficulty did the French ambassador succeed in preventing a step, which was as impolitic as it was disgraceful. Though on the whole, the result of the congress had fallen far short of Oxenstiern's expectations, he had at least gained for himself and his crown his main object, namely, the direction of the whole confederacy; he had also succeeded in strengthening the bond of union between the four upper circles, and obtained from the states a yearly contribution of two millions and a half of dollars, for the maintenance of the army.

These concessions on the part of the States, demanded some return from Sweden. A few weeks after the death of Gustavus Adolphus, sorrow ended the days of the unfortunate Elector Palatine. For eight months he had swelled the pomp of his protector's court, and expended on it the small remainder of his patrimony. He was, at last, approaching the goal of his wishes, and the prospect of a brighter future was opening, when death deprived him of his protector. But what he regarded as the greatest calamity, was highly favourable to his heirs. Gustavus might venture to delay the restoration of his dominions, or to load the gift with hard conditions; but Oxenstiern, to whom the friendship of England, Holland, and Brandenburg, and the good opinion of the Reformed States were indispensable, felt the necessity of immediately fulfilling the obligations of justice. At this assembly, at Heilbronn, therefore, he engaged to surrender to Frederick's heirs the whole Palatinate, both the part already conquered, and that which remained to be conquered, with the exception of Manheim, which the Swedes were to hold, until they should be indemnified for their expenses. The Chancellor did not confine his liberality to the family of the Palatine alone; the other allied princes received proofs, though at a later period, of the gratitude of Sweden, which, however, she dispensed at little cost to herself.

Impartiality, the most sacred obligation of the historian, here compels us to an admission, not much to the honour of the champions of German liberty. However the Protestant Princes might boast of the justice of their cause, and the sincerity of their conviction, still the motives from which they acted were selfish enough; and the desire of stripping others of their possessions, had at least as great a share in the commencement of hostilities, as the fear of being deprived of their own. Gustavus soon found that he might reckon much more on these selfish motives, than on their patriotic zeal, and did not fail to avail himself of them. Each of his confederates received from him the promise of some possession, either already wrested, or to be afterwards taken from the enemy; and death alone prevented him from fulfilling these engagements. What prudence had suggested to the king, necessity now prescribed to his successor. If it was his object to continue the war, he must be ready to divide the spoil among the allies, and promise them advantages from the confusion which it was his object to continue. Thus he promised to the Landgrave of Hesse, the abbacies of Paderborn, Corvey, Munster, and Fulda; to Duke Bernard of Weimar, the Franconian Bishoprics; to the Duke of Wirtemberg, the Ecclesiastical domains, and the Austrian counties lying within his territories, all under the title of fiefs of Sweden. This spectacle, so strange and so dishonourable to the German character, surprised the Chancellor, who found it difficult to repress his contempt, and on one occasion exclaimed, "Let it be writ in our records, for an everlasting memorial, that a German prince made such a request of a Swedish nobleman, and that the Swedish nobleman granted it to the German upon German ground!"

After these successful measures, he was in a condition to take the field, and prosecute the war with fresh vigour. Soon after the victory at Lutzen, the troops of Saxony and Lunenburg united with the Swedish main body; and the Imperialists were, in a short time, totally driven from Saxony. The united army again divided: the Saxons marched towards Lusatia and Silesia, to act in conjunction with Count Thurn against the Austrians in that quarter; a part of the Swedish army was led by the Duke of Weimar into Franconia, and the other by George, Duke of Brunswick, into Westphalia and Lower Saxony.

The conquests on the Lech and the Danube, during Gustavus's expedition into Saxony, had been maintained by the Palatine of Birkenfeld, and the Swedish General Banner, against the Bavarians; but unable to hold their ground against the victorious progress of the latter, supported as they were by the bravery and military experience of the Imperial General Altringer, they were under the necessity of summoning the Swedish General Horn to their assistance, from Alsace. This experienced general having captured the towns of Benfeld, Schlettstadt, Colmar, and Hagenau, committed the defence of them to the Rhinegrave Otto Louis, and hastily crossed the Rhine to form a junction with Banner's army. But although the combined force amounted to more than 16,000, they could not prevent the enemy from obtaining a strong position on the Swabian frontier, taking Kempten, and being joined by seven regiments from Bohemia. In order to retain the command of the important banks of the Lech and the Danube, they were under the necessity of recalling the Rhinegrave Otto Louis from Alsace, where he had, after the departure of Horn, found it difficult to defend himself against the exasperated peasantry. With his army, he was now summoned to strengthen the army on the Danube; and as even this reinforcement was insufficient, Duke Bernard of Weimar was earnestly pressed to turn his arms into this quarter.

Duke Bernard, soon after the opening of the campaign of 1633, had made himself master of the town and territory of Bamberg, and was now threatening Wurtzburg. But on receiving the summons of

General Horn, without delay he began his march towards the Danube, defeated on his way a Bavarian army under John de Werth, and joined the Swedes near Donauwerth. This numerous force, commanded by excellent generals, now threatened Bavaria with a fearful inroad. The bishopric of Eichstadt was completely overrun, and Ingoldstadt was on the point of being delivered up by treachery to the Swedes. Altringer, fettered in his movements by the express order of the Duke of Friedland, and left without assistance from Bohemia, was unable to check the progress of the enemy. The most favourable circumstances combined to further the progress of the Swedish arms in this quarter, when the operations of the army were at once stopped by a mutiny among the officers.

All the previous successes in Germany were owing altogether to arms; the greatness of Gustavus himself was the work of the army, the fruit of their discipline, their bravery, and their persevering courage under numberless dangers and privations. However wisely his plans were laid in the cabinet, it was to the army ultimately that he was indebted for their execution; and the expanding designs of the general did but continually impose new burdens on the soldiers. All the decisive advantages of the war, had been violently gained by a barbarous sacrifice of the soldiers' lives in winter campaigns, forced marches, stormings, and pitched battles; for it was Gustavus's maxim never to decline a battle, so long as it cost him nothing but men. The soldiers could not long be kept ignorant of their own importance, and they justly demanded a share in the spoil which had been won by their own blood. Yet, frequently, they hardly received their pay; and the rapacity of individual generals, or the wants of the state, generally swallowed up the greater part of the sums raised by contributions, or levied upon the conquered provinces. For all the privations he endured, the soldier had no other recompense than the doubtful chance either of plunder or promotion, in both of which he was often disappointed. During the lifetime of Gustavus Adolphus, the combined influence of fear and hope had suppressed any open complaint, but after his death, the murmurs were loud and universal; and the soldiery seized the most dangerous moment to impress their superiors with a sense of their importance. Two officers, Pfuhl and Mitschefal, notorious as restless characters, even during the King's life, set the example in the camp on the Danube, which in a few days was imitated by almost all the officers of the army. They solemnly bound themselves to obey no orders, till these arrears, now outstanding for months, and even years, should be paid up, and a gratuity, either in money or lands, made to each man, according to his services. "Immense sums," they said, "were daily raised by contributions, and all dissipated by a few. They were called out to serve amidst frost and snow, and no reward requited their incessant labours. The soldiers' excesses at Heilbronn had been blamed, but no one ever talked of their services. The world rung with the tidings of conquests and victories, but it was by their hands that they had been fought and won."

The number of the malcontents daily increased; and they even attempted by letters, (which were fortunately intercepted,) to seduce the armies on the Rhine and in Saxony. Neither the representations of Bernard of Weimar, nor the stern reproaches of his harsher associate in command, could suppress this mutiny, while the vehemence of Horn seemed only to increase the insolence of the insurgents. The conditions they insisted on, were that certain towns should be assigned to each regiment for the payment of arrears. Four weeks were allowed to the Swedish Chancellor to comply with these demands; and in case of refusal, they announced that they would pay themselves, and never more draw a sword for Sweden.

These pressing demands, made at the very time when the military chest was exhausted, and credit at a low ebb, greatly embarrassed the chancellor. The remedy, he saw, must be found quickly, before the contagion should spread to the other troops, and he should be deserted by all his armies at once. Among all the Swedish generals, there was only one of sufficient authority and influence with the soldiers to put an end to this dispute. The Duke of Weimar was the favourite of the army, and his prudent moderation had won the good-will of the soldiers, while his military experience had excited their admiration. He now undertook the task of appeasing the discontented troops; but, aware of his importance, he embraced the opportunity to make advantageous stipulations for himself, and to make the embarrassment of the chancellor subservient to his own views.

Gustavus Adolphus had flattered him with the promise of the Duchy of Franconia, to be formed out of the Bishoprics of Wurtzburg and Bamberg, and he now insisted on the performance of this pledge. He at the same time demanded the chief command, as generalissimo of Sweden. The abuse which the Duke of Weimar thus made of his influence, so irritated Oxenstiern, that, in the first moment of his displeasure, he gave him his dismissal from the Swedish service. But he soon thought better of it, and determined, instead of sacrificing so important a leader, to attach him to the Swedish interests at any cost. He therefore granted to him the Franconian bishoprics, as a fief of the Swedish crown, reserving, however, the two fortresses of Wurtzburg and Koenigshofen, which were to be garrisoned by the Swedes; and also engaged, in name of the Swedish crown, to secure these territories to the duke. His demand of the supreme authority was evaded on some specious pretext. The duke did not delay to display his gratitude for this valuable grant, and by his influence and activity soon restored tranquillity to the army. Large sums of money, and still more extensive estates, were divided among the officers, amounting in value to about five millions of dollars, and to which they had no other right but that of conquest. In the mean time, however, the opportunity for a great undertaking had been lost, and the united generals divided their forces to oppose the enemy in other quarters.

Gustavus Horn, after a short inroad into the Upper Palatinate, and the capture of Neumark, directed his march towards the Swabian frontier, where the Imperialists, strongly reinforced, threatened Wuertemberg. At his approach, the enemy retired to the Lake of Constance, but only to show the Swedes the road into a district hitherto unvisited by war. A post on the entrance to Switzerland, would be highly serviceable to the Swedes, and the town of Kostnitz seemed peculiarly well fitted to be a point of communication between him and the confederated cantons. Accordingly, Gustavus Horn immediately commenced the siege of it; but destitute of artillery, for which he was obliged to send to Wirtemberg, he could not press the attack with sufficient vigour, to prevent the enemy from throwing supplies into the town, which the lake afforded them convenient opportunity of doing. He, therefore, after an ineffectual attempt, quitted the place and its neighbourhood, and hastened to meet a more threatening danger upon the Danube.

At the Emperor's instigation, the Cardinal Infante, the brother of Philip IV. of Spain, and the Viceroy of Milan, had raised an army of 14,000 men, intended to act upon the Rhine, independently of Wallenstein, and to protect Alsace. This force now appeared in Bavaria, under the command of the Duke of Feria, a Spaniard; and, that they might be directly employed against the Swedes, Altringer was ordered to join them with his corps. Upon the first intelligence of their approach, Horn had summoned to his assistance the Palsgrave of Birkenfeld, from the Rhine; and being joined by him at Stockach, boldly advanced to meet the enemy's army of 30,000 men.

The latter had taken the route across the Danube into Swabia, where Gustavus Horn came so close upon them, that the two armies were only separated from each other by half a German mile. But, instead of accepting the offer of battle, the Imperialists moved by the Forest towns towards Briesgau and Alsace, where they arrived in time to relieve Breysack, and to arrest the victorious progress of the Rhinegrave, Otto Louis. The latter had, shortly before, taken the Forest towns, and, supported by the Palatine of Birkenfeld, who had liberated the Lower Palatinate and beaten the Duke of Lorraine out of the field, had once more given the superiority to the Swedish arms in that quarter. He was now forced to retire before the superior numbers of the enemy; but Horn and Birkenfeld quickly advanced to his support, and the Imperialists, after a brief triumph, were again expelled from Alsace. The severity of the autumn, in which this hapless retreat had to be conducted, proved fatal to most of the Italians; and their leader, the Duke of Feria, died of grief at the failure of his enterprise.

In the mean time, Duke Bernard of Weimar had taken up his position on the Danube, with eighteen regiments of infantry and 140 squadrons of horse, to cover Franconia, and to watch the movements of the Imperial-Bavarian army upon that river. No sooner had Altringer departed, to join the Italians under Feria, than Bernard, profiting by his absence, hastened across the Danube, and with the rapidity of lightning appeared before Ratisbon. The possession of this town would ensure the success of the Swedish designs upon Bavaria and Austria; it would establish them firmly on the Danube, and provide a safe refuge in case of defeat, while it alone could give permanence to their conquests in that quarter. To defend Ratisbon, was the urgent advice which the dying Tilly left to the Elector; and Gustavus Adolphus had lamented it as an irreparable loss, that the Bavarians had anticipated him in taking possession of this place. Indescribable, therefore, was the consternation of Maximilian, when Duke Bernard suddenly appeared before the town, and prepared in earnest to besiege it.

The garrison consisted of not more than fifteen companies, mostly newly-raised soldiers; although that number was more than sufficient to weary out an enemy of far superior force, if supported by well-disposed and warlike inhabitants. But this was not the greatest danger which the Bavarian garrison had to contend against. The Protestant inhabitants of Ratisbon, equally jealous of their civil and religious freedom, had unwillingly submitted to the yoke of Bavaria, and had long looked with impatience for the appearance of a deliverer. Bernard's arrival before the walls filled them with lively joy; and there was much reason to fear that they would support the attempts of the besiegers without, by exciting a tumult within. In this perplexity, the Elector addressed the most pressing entreaties to the Emperor and the Duke of Friedland to assist him, were it only with 5,000 men. Seven messengers in succession were despatched by Ferdinand to Wallenstein, who promised immediate succours, and even announced to the Elector the near advance of 12,000 men under Gallas; but at the same time forbade that general, under pain of death, to march. Meanwhile the Bavarian commandant of Ratisbon, in the hope of speedy assistance, made the best preparations for defence, armed the Roman Catholic peasants, disarmed and carefully watched the Protestant citizens, lest they should attempt any hostile design against the garrison. But as no relief arrived, and the enemy's artillery incessantly battered the walls, he consulted his own safety, and that of the garrison, by an honourable capitulation, and abandoned the Bavarian officials and ecclesiastics to the conqueror's mercy.

The possession of Ratisbon, enlarged the projects of the duke, and Bavaria itself now appeared too narrow a field for his bold designs. He determined to penetrate to the frontiers of Austria, to arm the

Protestant peasantry against the Emperor, and restore to them their religious liberty. He had already taken Straubingen, while another Swedish army was advancing successfully along the northern bank of the Danube. At the head of his Swedes, bidding defiance to the severity of the weather, he reached the mouth of the Iser, which he passed in the presence of the Bavarian General Werth, who was encamped on that river. Passau and Lintz trembled for their fate; the terrified Emperor redoubled his entreaties and commands to Wallenstein, to hasten with all speed to the relief of the hard-pressed Bavarians. But here the victorious Bernard, of his own accord, checked his career of conquest. Having in front of him the river Inn, guarded by a number of strong fortresses, and behind him two hostile armies, a disaffected country, and the river Iser, while his rear was covered by no tenable position, and no entrenchment could be made in the frozen ground, and threatened by the whole force of Wallenstein, who had at last resolved to march to the Danube, by a timely retreat he escaped the danger of being cut off from Ratisbon, and surrounded by the enemy. He hastened across the Iser to the Danube, to defend the conquests he had made in the Upper Palatinate against Wallenstein, and fully resolved not to decline a battle, if necessary, with that general. But Wallenstein, who was not disposed for any great exploits on the Danube, did not wait for his approach; and before the Bavarians could congratulate themselves on his arrival, he suddenly withdrew again into Bohemia. The duke thus ended his victorious campaign, and allowed his troops their well-earned repose in winter quarters upon an enemy's country.

While in Swabia the war was thus successfully conducted by Gustavus Horn, and on the Upper and Lower Rhine by the Palatine of Birkenfeld, General Baudissen, and the Rhinegrave Otto Louis, and by Duke Bernard on the Danube; the reputation of the Swedish arms was as gloriously sustained in Lower Saxony and Westphalia by the Duke of Lunenburg and the Landgrave of Hesse Cassel. The fortress of Hamel was taken by Duke George, after a brave defence, and a brilliant victory obtained over the imperial General Gronsfeld, by the united Swedish and Hessian armies, near Oldendorf. Count Wasaburg, a natural son of Gustavus Adolphus, showed himself in this battle worthy of his descent. Sixteen pieces of cannon, the whole baggage of the Imperialists, together with 74 colours, fell into the hands of the Swedes; 3,000 of the enemy perished on the field, and nearly the same number were taken prisoners. The town of Osnaburg surrendered to the Swedish Colonel Knyphausen, and Paderborn to the Landgrave of Hesse; while, on the other hand, Bueckeburg, a very important place for the Swedes, fell into the hands of the Imperialists. The Swedish banners were victorious in almost every quarter of Germany; and the year after the death of Gustavus, left no trace of the loss which had been sustained in the person of that great leader.

In a review of the important events which signalized the campaign of 1633, the inactivity of a man, of whom the highest expectations had been formed, justly excites astonishment. Among all the generals who distinguished themselves in this campaign, none could be compared with Wallenstein, in experience, talents, and reputation; and yet, after the battle of Lutzen, we lose sight of him entirely. The fall of his great rival had left the whole theatre of glory open to him; all Europe was now attentively awaiting those exploits, which should efface the remembrance of his defeat, and still prove to the world his military superiority. Nevertheless, he continued inactive in Bohemia, while the Emperor's losses in Bavaria, Lower Saxony, and the Rhine, pressingly called for his presence—a conduct equally unintelligible to friend and foe—the terror, and, at the same time, the last hope of the Emperor. After the defeat of Lutzen he had hastened into Bohemia, where he instituted the strictest inquiry into the conduct of his officers in that battle. Those whom the council of war declared guilty of misconduct, were put to death without mercy, those who had behaved with bravery, rewarded with princely munificence, and the memory of the dead honoured by splendid monuments. During the winter, he oppressed the imperial provinces by enormous contributions, and exhausted the Austrian territories by his winter quarters, which he purposely avoided taking up in an enemy's country. And in the spring of 1633, instead of being the first to open the campaign, with this well-chosen and well-appointed army, and to make a worthy display of his great abilities, he was the last who appeared in the field; and even then, it was an hereditary province of Austria, which he selected as the seat of war.

Of all the Austrian provinces, Silesia was most exposed to danger. Three different armies, a Swedish under Count Thurn, a Saxon under Arnheim and the Duke of Lauenburg, and one of Brandenburg under Borgsdorf, had at the same time carried the war into this country; they had already taken possession of the most important places, and even Breslau had embraced the cause of the allies. But this crowd of commanders and armies was the very means of saving this province to the Emperor; for the jealousy of the generals, and the mutual hatred of the Saxons and the Swedes, never allowed them to act with unanimity. Arnheim and Thurn contended for the chief command; the troops of Brandenburg and Saxony combined against the Swedes, whom they looked upon as troublesome strangers who ought to be got rid of as soon as possible. The Saxons, on the contrary, lived on a very intimate footing with the Imperialists, and the officers of both these hostile armies often visited and entertained each other. The Imperialists were allowed to remove their property without hindrance, and many did not affect to conceal that they had received large sums from Vienna. Among such equivocal allies, the Swedes saw themselves sold and betrayed; and any great enterprise was out of the question, while so bad an understanding prevailed between the troops. General Arnheim, too, was absent the greater part of the time; and when he at last returned, Wallenstein was fast approaching the frontiers with a formidable force.

His army amounted to 40,000 men, while to oppose him the allies had only 24,000. They nevertheless resolved to give him battle, and marched to Munsterberg, where he had formed an intrenched camp. But Wallenstein remained inactive for eight days; he then left his intrenchments, and marched slowly and with composure to the enemy's camp. But even after quitting his position, and when the enemy, emboldened by his past delay, manfully prepared to receive him, he declined the opportunity of fighting. The caution with which he avoided a battle was imputed to fear; but the well-established reputation of Wallenstein enabled him to despise this suspicion. The vanity of the allies allowed them not to see that he purposely saved them a defeat, because a victory at that time would not have served his own ends. To convince them of his superior power, and that his inactivity proceeded not from any fear of them, he put to death the commander of a castle that fell into his hands, because he had refused at once to surrender an untenable place.

For nine days, did the two armies remain within musket-shot of each other, when Count Terzky, from the camp of the Imperialists, appeared with a trumpeter in that of the allies, inviting General Arnheim to a conference. The purport was, that Wallenstein, notwithstanding his superiority, was willing to agree to a cessation of arms for six weeks. "He was come," he said, "to conclude a lasting peace with the Swedes, and with the princes of the empire, to pay the soldiers, and to satisfy every one. All this was in his power; and if the Austrian court hesitated to confirm his agreement, he would unite with the allies, and (as he privately whispered to Arnheim) hunt the Emperor to the devil." At the second conference, he expressed himself still more plainly to Count Thurn. "All the privileges of the Bohemians," he engaged, "should be confirmed anew, the exiles recalled and restored to their estates, and he himself would be the first to resign his share of them. The Jesuits, as the authors of all past grievances, should be banished, the Swedish crown indemnified by stated payments, and all the superfluous troops on both sides employed against the Turks." The last article explained the whole mystery. "If," he continued, "HE should obtain the crown of Bohemia, all the exiles would have reason to applaud his generosity; perfect toleration of religions should be established within the kingdom, the Palatine family be reinstated in its rights, and he would accept the Margraviate of Moravia as a compensation for Mecklenburg. The allied armies would then, under his command, advance upon Vienna, and sword in hand, compel the Emperor to ratify the treaty."

Thus was the veil at last removed from the schemes, over which he had brooded for years in mysterious silence. Every circumstance now convinced him that not a moment was to be lost in its execution. Nothing but a blind confidence in the good fortune and military genius of the Duke of Friedland, had induced the Emperor, in the face of the remonstrances of Bavaria and Spain, and at the expense of his own reputation, to confer upon this imperious leader such an unlimited command. But this belief in Wallenstein's being invincible, had been much weakened by his inaction, and almost entirely overthrown by the defeat at Lutzen. His enemies at the imperial court now renewed their intrigues; and the Emperor's disappointment at the failure of his hopes, procured for their remonstrances a favourable reception. Wallenstein's whole conduct was now reviewed with the most malicious criticism; his ambitious haughtiness, his disobedience to the Emperor's orders, were recalled to the recollection of that jealous prince, as well as the complaints of the Austrian subjects against his boundless oppression; his fidelity was questioned, and alarming hints thrown out as to his secret views. These insinuations, which the conduct of the duke seemed but too well to justify, failed not to make a deep impression on Ferdinand; but the step had been taken, and the great power with which Wallenstein had been invested, could not be taken from him without danger. Insensibly to diminish that power, was the only course that now remained, and, to effect this, it must in the first place be divided; but, above all, the Emperor's present dependence on the good will of his general put an end to. But even this right had been resigned in his engagement with Wallenstein, and the Emperor's own handwriting secured him against every attempt to unite another general with him in the command, or to exercise any immediate act of authority over the troops. As this disadvantageous contract could neither be kept nor broken, recourse was had to artifice. Wallenstein was Imperial Generalissimo in Germany, but his command extended no further, and he could not presume to exercise any authority over a foreign army. A Spanish army was accordingly raised in Milan, and marched into Germany under a Spanish general. Wallenstein now ceased to be indispensable because he was no longer supreme, and in case of necessity, the Emperor was now provided with the means of support even against him.

The duke quickly and deeply felt whence this blow came, and whither it was aimed. In vain did he protest against this violation of the compact, to the Cardinal Infante; the Italian army continued its march, and he was forced to detach General Altringer to join it with a reinforcement. He took care, indeed, so closely to fetter the latter, as to prevent the Italian army from acquiring any great reputation in Alsace and Swabia; but this bold step of the court awakened him from his security, and warned him of the approach of danger. That he might not a second time be deprived of his command, and lose the fruit of all his labours, he must accelerate the accomplishment of his long meditated designs. He secured the attachment of his troops by removing the doubtful officers, and by his liberality to the rest. He had sacrificed to the welfare of the army every other order in the state, every consideration of justice and humanity, and therefore he reckoned upon their gratitude. At the very moment when he meditated an unparalleled act of ingratitude against the author of his own good fortune, he founded all his hopes upon the gratitude which was due to himself.

The leaders of the Silesian armies had no authority from their principals to consent, on their own discretion, to such important proposals as those of Wallenstein, and they did not even feel themselves warranted in granting, for more than a fortnight, the cessation of hostilities which he demanded. Before the duke disclosed his designs to Sweden and Saxony, he had deemed it advisable to secure the sanction of France to his bold undertaking. For this purpose, a secret negociation had been carried on with the greatest possible caution and distrust, by Count Kinsky with Feuquieres, the French ambassador at Dresden, and had terminated according to his wishes. Feuquieres received orders from his court to promise every assistance on the part of France, and to offer the duke a considerable pecuniary aid in case of need.

But it was this excessive caution to secure himself on all sides, that led to his ruin. The French ambassador with astonishment discovered that a plan, which, more than any other, required secrecy, had been communicated to the Swedes and the Saxons. And yet it was generally known that the Saxon ministry was in the interests of the Emperor, and on the other hand, the conditions offered to the Swedes fell too far short of their expectations to be likely to be accepted. Feuquieres, therefore, could not believe that the duke could be serious in calculating upon the aid of the latter, and the silence of the former. He communicated accordingly his doubts and anxieties to the Swedish chancellor, who equally distrusted the views of Wallenstein, and disliked his plans. Although it was no secret to Oxenstiern, that the duke had formerly entered into a similar negociation with Gustavus Adolphus, he could not credit the possibility of inducing a whole army to revolt, and of his extravagant promises. So daring a design, and such imprudent conduct, seemed not to be consistent with the duke's reserved and suspicious temper, and he was the more inclined to consider the whole as the result of dissimulation and treachery, because he had less reason to doubt his prudence than his honesty.

Oxenstiern's doubts at last affected Arnheim himself, who, in full confidence in Wallenstein's sincerity, had repaired to the chancellor at Gelnhausen, to persuade him to lend some of his best regiments to the duke, to aid him in the execution of the plan. They began to suspect that the whole proposal was only a snare to disarm the allies, and to betray the flower of their troops into the hands of the Emperor. Wallenstein's well-known character did not contradict the suspicion, and the inconsistencies in which he afterwards involved himself, entirely destroyed all confidence in his sincerity. While he was endeavouring to draw the Swedes into this alliance, and requiring the help of their best troops, he declared to Arnheim that they must begin with expelling the Swedes from the empire; and while the Saxon officers, relying upon the security of the truce, repaired in great numbers to his camp, he made an unsuccessful attempt to seize them. He was the first to break the truce, which some months afterwards he renewed, though not without great difficulty. All confidence in his sincerity was lost; his whole conduct was regarded as a tissue of deceit and low cunning, devised to weaken the allies and repair his own strength. This indeed he actually did effect, as his own army daily augmented, while that of the allies was reduced nearly one half by desertion and bad provisions. But he did not make that use of his superiority which Vienna expected. When all men were looking for a decisive blow to be struck, he suddenly renewed the negociations; and when the truce lulled the allies into security, he as suddenly recommenced hostilities. All these contradictions arose out of the double and irreconcileable designs to ruin at once the Emperor and the Swedes, and to conclude a separate peace with the Saxons.

Impatient at the ill success of his negociations, he at last determined to display his strength; the more so, as the pressing distress within the empire, and the growing dissatisfaction of the Imperial court, admitted not of his making any longer delay. Before the last cessation of hostilities, General Holk, from Bohemia, had attacked the circle of Meissen, laid waste every thing on his route with fire and sword, driven the Elector into his fortresses, and taken the town of Leipzig. But the truce in Silesia put a period to his ravages, and the consequences of his excesses brought him to the grave at Adorf. As soon as hostilities were recommenced, Wallenstein made a movement, as if he designed to penetrate through Lusatia into Saxony, and circulated the report that Piccolomini had already invaded that country. Arnheim immediately broke up his camp in Silesia, to follow him, and hastened to the assistance of the Electorate. By this means the Swedes were left exposed, who were encamped in small force under Count Thurn, at Steinau, on the Oder, and this was exactly what Wallenstein desired. He allowed the Saxon general to advance sixteen miles towards Meissen, and then suddenly turning towards the Oder, surprised the Swedish army in the most complete security. Their cavalry were first beaten by General Schafgotsch, who was sent against them, and the infantry completely surrounded at Steinau by the duke's army which followed. Wallenstein gave Count Thurn half an hour to deliberate whether he would defend himself with 2,500 men, against more than 20,000, or surrender at discretion. But there was no room for deliberation. The army surrendered, and the most complete victory was obtained without bloodshed. Colours, baggage, and artillery all fell into the hands of the victors, the officers were taken into custody, the privates drafted into the army of Wallenstein. And now at last, after a banishment of fourteen years, after numberless changes of fortune, the author of the Bohemian insurrection, and the remote origin of this destructive war, the notorious Count Thurn, was in the power of his enemies. With blood-thirsty impatience, the arrival of this great criminal was looked for in Vienna, where they already anticipated the malicious triumph of sacrificing so distinguished a victim to public justice. But to deprive the Jesuits of this pleasure, was a still sweeter triumph to Wallenstein, and Thurn was set at liberty. Fortunately for him, he knew more than it was prudent to have divulged in Vienna, and his enemies were also those of Wallenstein. A defeat might have been forgiven in Vienna, but this disappointment of their hopes they could not pardon. "What should I have done with this madman?" he writes, with a malicious sneer, to the minister who called him to account for this unseasonable magnanimity. "Would to Heaven the enemy had no generals but such as he. At the head of the Swedish army, he will render us much better service than in prison."

The victory of Steinau was followed by the capture of Liegnitz, Grossglogau, and even of Frankfort on the Oder. Schafgotsch, who remained in Silesia to complete the subjugation of that province, blockaded Brieg, and threatened Breslau, though in vain, as that free town was jealous of its privileges, and devoted to the Swedes. Colonels Illo and Goetz were ordered by Wallenstein to the Warta, to push forwards into Pomerania, and to the coasts of the Baltic, and actually obtained possession of Landsberg, the key of Pomerania. While thus the Elector of Brandenburg and the Duke of Pomerania were made to tremble for their dominions, Wallenstein himself, with the remainder of his army, burst suddenly into Lusatia, where he took Goerlitz by storm, and forced Bautzen to surrender. But his object was merely to alarm the Elector of Saxony, not to follow up the advantages already obtained; and therefore, even with the sword in his hand, he continued his negociations for peace with Brandenburg and Saxony, but with no better success than before, as the inconsistencies of his conduct had destroyed all confidence in his sincerity. He was therefore on the point of turning his whole force in earnest against the unfortunate Saxons, and effecting his object by force of arms, when circumstances compelled him to leave these territories. The conquests of Duke Bernard upon the Danube, which threatened Austria itself with immediate danger, urgently demanded his presence in Bavaria; and the expulsion of the Saxons and Swedes from Silesia, deprived him of every pretext for longer resisting the Imperial orders, and leaving the Elector of Bavaria without assistance. With his main body, therefore, he immediately set out for the Upper Palatinate, and his retreat freed Upper Saxony for ever of this formidable enemy.

So long as was possible, he had delayed to move to the rescue of Bavaria, and on every pretext evaded the commands of the Emperor. He had, indeed, after reiterated remonstrances, despatched from Bohemia a reinforcement of some regiments to Count Altringer, who was defending the Lech and the Danube against Horn and Bernard, but under the express condition of his acting merely on the defensive. He referred the Emperor and the Elector, whenever they applied to him for aid, to Altringer, who, as he publicly gave out, had received unlimited powers; secretly, however, he tied up his hands by the strictest injunctions, and even threatened him with death, if he exceeded his orders. When Duke Bernard had appeared before Ratisbon, and the Emperor as well as the Elector repeated still more urgently their demand for succour, he pretended he was about to despatch General Gallas with a considerable army to the Danube; but this movement also was delayed, and Ratisbon, Straubing, and Cham, as well as the bishopric of Eichstaedt, fell into the hands of the Swedes. When at last he could no longer neglect the orders of the Court, he marched slowly toward the Bavarian frontier, where he invested the town of Cham, which had been taken by the Swedes. But no sooner did he learn that on the Swedish side a diversion was contemplated, by an inroad of the Saxons into Bohemia, than he availed himself of the report, as a pretext for immediately retreating into that kingdom. Every consideration, he urged, must be postponed to the defence and preservation of the hereditary dominions of the Emperor; and on this plea, he remained firmly fixed in Bohemia, which he guarded as if it had been his own property. And when the Emperor laid upon him his commands to move towards the Danube, and prevent the Duke of Weimar from establishing himself in so dangerous a position on the frontiers of Austria, Wallenstein thought proper to conclude the campaign a second time, and quartered his troops for the winter in this exhausted kingdom.

Such continued insolence and unexampled contempt of the Imperial orders, as well as obvious neglect of the common cause, joined to his equivocal behaviour towards the enemy, tended at last to convince the Emperor of the truth of those unfavourable reports with regard to the Duke, which were current through Germany. The latter had, for a long time, succeeded in glozing over his criminal correspondence with the enemy, and persuading the Emperor, still prepossessed in his favour, that the sole object of his secret conferences was to obtain peace for Germany. But impenetrable as he himself believed his proceedings to be, in the course of his conduct, enough transpired to justify the insinuations with which his rivals incessantly loaded the ear of the Emperor. In order to satisfy himself of the truth or falsehood of these rumours, Ferdinand had already, at different times, sent spies into Wallenstein's camp; but as the Duke took the precaution never to commit anything to writing, they returned with nothing but conjectures. But when, at last, those ministers who formerly had been his champions at the court, in consequence of their estates not being exempted by Wallenstein from the general exactions, joined his enemies; when the Elector of Bavaria threatened, in case of Wallenstein being any longer retained in the supreme command, to unite with the Swedes; when the Spanish ambassador insisted on his dismissal, and threatened, in case of refusal, to withdraw the subsidies furnished by his Crown, the Emperor found himself a second time compelled to deprive him of the command.

The Emperor's authoritative and direct interference with the army, soon convinced the Duke that the compact with himself was regarded as at an end, and that his dismissal was inevitable. One of his inferior generals in Austria, whom he had forbidden, under pain of death, to obey the orders of the court, received the positive commands of the Emperor to join the Elector of Bavaria; and Wallenstein himself was imperiously ordered to send some regiments to reinforce the army of the Cardinal Infante, who was on his march from Italy. All these measures convinced him that the plan was finally arranged to disarm him by degrees, and at once, when he was weak and defenceless, to complete his ruin.

In self-defence, must he now hasten to carry into execution the plans which he had originally formed only with the view to aggrandizement. He had delayed too long, either because the favourable configuration of the stars had not yet presented itself, or, as he used to say, to check the impatience of his friends, because THE TIME WAS NOT YET COME. The time, even now, was not come: but the pressure of circumstances no longer allowed him to await the favour of the stars. The first step was to assure himself of the sentiments of his principal officers, and then to try the attachment of the army, which he had so long confidently reckoned on. Three of them, Colonels Kinsky, Terzky, and Illo, had long been in his secrets, and the two first were further united to his interests by the ties of relationship. The same wild ambition, the same bitter hatred of the government, and the hope of enormous rewards, bound them in the closest manner to Wallenstein, who, to increase the number of his adherents, could stoop to the lowest means. He had once advised Colonel Illo to solicit, in Vienna, the title of Count, and had promised to back his application with his powerful mediation. But he secretly wrote to the ministry, advising them to refuse his request, as to grant it would give rise to similar demands from others, whose services and claims were equal to his. On Illo's return to the camp, Wallenstein immediately demanded to know the success of his mission; and when informed by Illo of its failure, he broke out into the bitterest complaints against the court. "Thus," said he, "are our faithful services rewarded. My recommendation is disregarded, and your merit denied so trifling a reward! Who would any longer devote his services to so ungrateful a master? No, for my part, I am henceforth the determined foe of Austria." Illo agreed with him, and a close alliance was cemented between them.

But what was known to these three confidants of the duke, was long an impenetrable secret to the rest; and the confidence with which Wallenstein spoke of the devotion of his officers, was founded merely on the favours he had lavished on them, and on their known dissatisfaction with the Court. But this vague presumption must be converted into certainty, before he could venture to lay aside the mask, or take any open step against the Emperor. Count Piccolomini, who had distinguished himself by his unparalleled bravery at Lutzen, was the first whose fidelity he put to the proof. He had, he thought, gained the attachment of this general by large presents, and preferred him to all others, because born under the same constellations with himself. He disclosed to him, that, in consequence of the Emperor's ingratitude, and the near approach of his own danger, he had irrevocably determined entirely to abandon the party of Austria, to join the enemy with the best part of his army, and to make war upon the House of Austria, on all sides of its dominions, till he had wholly extirpated it. In the execution of this plan, he principally reckoned on the services of Piccolomini, and had beforehand promised him the greatest rewards. When the latter, to conceal his amazement at this extraordinary communication, spoke of the dangers and obstacles which would oppose so hazardous an enterprise, Wallenstein ridiculed his fears. "In such enterprises," he maintained, "nothing was difficult but the commencement. The stars were propitious to him, the opportunity the best that could be wished for, and something must always be trusted to fortune. His resolution was taken, and if it could not be otherwise, he would encounter the hazard at the head of a thousand horse."

Piccolomini was careful not to excite Wallenstein's suspicions by longer opposition, and yielded apparently to the force of his reasoning. Such was the infatuation of the Duke, that notwithstanding the warnings of Count Terzky, he never doubted the sincerity of this man, who lost not a moment in communicating to the court at Vienna this important conversation.

Preparatory to taking the last decisive step, he, in January 1634, called a meeting of all the commanders of the army at Pilsen, whither he had marched after his retreat from Bavaria. The Emperor's recent orders to spare his hereditary dominions from winter quarterings, to recover Ratisbon in the middle of winter, and to reduce the army by a detachment of six thousand horse to the Cardinal Infante, were matters sufficiently grave to be laid before a council of war; and this plausible pretext served to conceal from the curious the real object of the meeting. Sweden and Saxony received invitations to be present, in order to treat with the Duke of Friedland for a peace; to the leaders of more distant armies, written communications were made. Of the commanders thus summoned, twenty appeared; but three most influential, Gallas, Colloredo, and Altringer, were absent. The Duke reiterated his summons to them, and in the mean time, in expectation of their speedy arrival, proceeded to execute his designs.

It was no light task that he had to perform: a nobleman, proud, brave, and jealous of his honour, was to declare himself capable of the basest treachery, in the very presence of those who had been accustomed to regard him as the representative of majesty, the judge of their actions, and the supporter of their laws, and to show himself suddenly as a traitor, a cheat, and a rebel. It was no easy task, either, to shake to its foundations a legitimate sovereignty, strengthened by time and consecrated by laws and religion; to dissolve all the charms of the senses and the imagination, those formidable guardians of an established throne, and to attempt forcibly to uproot those invincible feelings of duty, which plead so loudly and so powerfully in the breast of the subject, in favour of his sovereign. But, blinded by the splendour of a crown, Wallenstein observed not the precipice that yawned beneath his feet; and in full reliance on his own strength, the common case with energetic and daring minds, he stopped not to consider the magnitude and the number of the difficulties that opposed him. Wallenstein saw nothing but an army, partly indifferent and partly exasperated against the court, accustomed, with a blind submission, to do homage to his great name, to bow to him as their legislator and judge, and with trembling reverence to follow his orders as the decrees of fate. In the extravagant flatteries which were paid to his omnipotence, in the bold abuse of the court government, in which a lawless soldiery indulged, and which the wild licence of the camp excused, he thought he read the sentiments of the army; and the boldness with which they were ready to censure the monarch's measures, passed with him for a readiness to renounce their allegiance to a sovereign so little respected. But that which he had regarded as the lightest matter, proved the most formidable obstacle with which he had to contend; the soldiers' feelings of allegiance were the rock on which his hopes were wrecked. Deceived by the profound respect in which he was held by these lawless bands, he ascribed the whole to his own personal greatness, without distinguishing how much he owed to himself, and how much to the dignity with which he was invested. All trembled before him, while he exercised a legitimate authority, while obedience to him was a duty, and while his consequence was supported by the majesty of the sovereign. Greatness, in and of itself, may excite terror and admiration; but legitimate greatness alone can inspire reverence and submission; and of this decisive advantage he deprived himself, the instant he avowed himself a traitor.

Field-Marshal Illo undertook to learn the sentiments of the officers, and to prepare them for the step which was expected of them. He began by laying before them the new orders of the court to the general and the army; and by the obnoxious turn he skilfully gave to them, he found it easy to excite the indignation of the assembly. After this well chosen introduction, he expatiated with much eloquence upon the merits of the army and the general, and the ingratitude with which the Emperor was accustomed to requite them. "Spanish influence," he maintained, "governed the court; the ministry were in the pay of Spain; the Duke of Friedland alone had hitherto opposed this tyranny, and had thus drawn down upon himself the deadly enmity of the Spaniards. To remove him from the command, or to make away with him entirely," he continued, "had long been the end of their desires; and, until they could succeed in one or other, they endeavoured to abridge his power in the field. The command was to be placed in the hands of the King of Hungary, for no other reason than the better to promote the Spanish power in Germany; because this prince, as the ready instrument of foreign counsels, might be led at pleasure. It was merely with the view of weakening the army, that the six thousand troops were required for the Cardinal Infante; it was solely for the purpose of harassing it by a winter campaign, that they were now called on, in this inhospitable season, to undertake the recovery of Ratisbon. The means of subsistence were everywhere rendered difficult, while the Jesuits and the ministry enriched themselves with the sweat of the provinces, and squandered the money intended for the pay of the troops. The general, abandoned by the court, acknowledges his inability to keep his engagements to the army. For all the services which, for two and twenty years, he had rendered the House of Austria; for all the difficulties with which he had struggled; for all the treasures of his own, which he had expended in the imperial service, a second disgraceful dismissal awaited him. But he was resolved the matter should not come to this; he was determined voluntarily to resign the command, before it should be wrested from his hands; and this," continued the orator, "is what, through me, he now makes known to his officers. It was now for them to say whether it would be advisable to lose such a general. Let each consider who was to refund him the sums he had expended in the Emperor's service, and where he was now to reap the reward of their bravery, when he who was their evidence removed from the scene."

A universal cry, that they would not allow their general to be taken from them, interrupted the speaker. Four of the principal officers were deputed to lay before him the wish of the assembly, and earnestly to request that he would not leave the army. The duke made a show of resistance, and only yielded after the second deputation. This concession on his side, seemed to demand a return on theirs; as he engaged not to quit the service without the knowledge and consent of the generals, he required of them, on the other hand, a written promise to truly and firmly adhere to him, neither to separate nor to allow themselves to be separated from him, and to shed their last drop of blood in his defence. Whoever should break this covenant, was to be regarded as a perfidious traitor, and treated by the rest as a common enemy. The express condition which was added, "AS LONG AS WALLENSTEIN SHALL EMPLOY THE ARMY IN THE EMPEROR'S SERVICE," seemed to exclude all misconception, and none of the assembled generals hesitated at once to accede to a demand, apparently so innocent and so reasonable.

This document was publicly read before an entertainment, which Field-Marshal Illo had expressly prepared for the purpose; it was to be signed, after they rose from table. The host did his utmost to stupify his guests by strong potations; and it was not until he saw them affected with the wine, that he produced the paper for signature. Most of them wrote their names, without knowing what they were subscribing; a few only, more curious or more distrustful, read the paper over again, and discovered with astonishment that the clause "as long as Wallenstein shall employ the army for the Emperor's service" was omitted. Illo had, in fact, artfully contrived to substitute for the first another copy, in which these words were wanting. The trick was manifest, and many refused now to sign. Piccolomini, who had seen through the whole cheat, and had been present at this scene merely with the view of giving information of the whole to the court, forgot himself so far in his cups as to drink the Emperor's health. But Count Terzky now rose, and declared that all were perjured villains who should recede from their engagement. His menaces, the idea of the inevitable danger to which they who resisted any longer would be exposed, the example of the rest, and Illo's rhetoric, at last overcame their scruples; and the paper was signed by all without exception.

Wallenstein had now effected his purpose; but the unexpected resistance he had met with from the commanders roused him at last from the fond illusions in which he had hitherto indulged. Besides, most of the names were scrawled so illegibly, that some deceit was evidently intended. But instead of being recalled to his discretion by this warning, he gave vent to his injured pride in undignified complaints and reproaches. He assembled the generals the next day, and undertook personally to confirm the whole tenor of the agrecment which Illo had submitted to them the day before. After pouring out the bitterest reproaches and abuse against the court, he reminded them of their opposition to the proposition of the previous day, and declared that this circumstance had induced him to retract his own promise. The generals withdrew in silence and confusion; but after a short consultation in the antichamber, they returned to apologize for their late conduct, and offered to sign the paper anew.

Nothing now remained, but to obtain a similar assurance from the absent generals, or, on their refusal, to seize their persons. Wallenstein renewed his invitation to them, and earnestly urged them to hasten their arrival. But a rumour of the doings at Pilsen reached them on their journey, and suddenly stopped their further progress. Altringer, on pretence of sickness, remained in the strong fortress of Frauenberg. Gallas made his appearance, but merely with the design of better qualifying himself as an eyewitness, to keep the Emperor informed of all Wallenstein's proceedings. The intelligence which he and Piccolomini gave, at once converted the suspicions of the court into an alarming certainty. Similar disclosures, which were at the same time made from other quarters, left no room for farther doubt; and the sudden change of the commanders in Austria and Silesia, appeared to be the prelude to some important enterprise. The danger was pressing, and the remedy must be speedy, but the court was unwilling to proceed at once to the execution of the sentence, till the regular forms of justice were complied with. Secret instructions were therefore issued to the principal officers, on whose fidelity reliance could be placed, to seize the persons of the Duke of Friedland and of his two associates, Illo and Terzky, and keep them in close confinement, till they should have an opportunity of being heard, and of answering for their conduct; but if this could not be accomplished quietly, the public danger required that they should be taken dead or live. At the same time, General Gallas received a patent commission, by which these orders of the Emperor were made known to the colonels and officers, and the army was released from its obedience to the traitor, and placed under Lieutenant-General Gallas, till a new generalissimo could be appointed. In order to bring back the seduced and deluded to their duty, and not to drive the guilty to despair, a general amnesty was proclaimed, in regard to all offences against the imperial majesty committed at Pilsen.

General Gallas was not pleased with the honour which was done him. He was at Pilsen, under the eye of the person whose fate he was to dispose of; in the power of an enemy, who had a hundred eyes to watch his motions. If Wallenstein once discovered the secret of his commission, nothing could save him from the effects of his vengeance and despair. But if it was thus dangerous to be the secret depositary of such a commission, how much more so to execute it? The sentiments of the generals were uncertain; and it was at least doubtful whether, after the step they had taken, they would be ready to trust the Emperor's promises, and at once to abandon the brilliant expectations they had built upon Wallenstein's enterprise. It was also hazardous to attempt to lay hands on the person of a man who, till now, had been considered inviolable; who from long exercise of supreme power, and from habitual obedience, had become the object of deepest respect; who was invested with every attribute of outward majesty and inward greatness; whose very aspect inspired terror, and who by a nod disposed of life and death! To seize such a man, like a common criminal, in the midst of the guards by whom he was surrounded, and in a city apparently devoted to him; to convert the object of this deep and habitual veneration into a subject of compassion, or of contempt, was a commission calculated to make even the boldest hesitate. So deeply was fear and veneration for their general engraven in the breasts of the soldiers, that even the atrocious crime of high treason could not wholly eradicate these sentiments.

Gallas perceived the impossibility of executing his commission under the eyes of the duke; and his most anxious wish was, before venturing on any steps, to have an interview with Altringer. As the long absence of the latter had already begun to excite the duke's suspicions, Gallas offered to repair in person to Frauenberg, and to prevail on Altringer, his relation, to return with him. Wallenstein was so pleased with this proof of his zeal, that he even lent him his own equipage for the journey. Rejoicing at the success of his stratagem, he left Pilsen without delay, leaving to Count Piccolomini the task of watching Wallenstein's further movements. He did not fail, as he went along, to make use of the imperial patent, and the sentiments of the troops proved more favourable than he had expected. Instead of taking back his friend to Pilsen, he despatched him to Vienna, to warn the Emperor against the intended attack, while he himself repaired to Upper Austria, of which the safety was threatened by the near approach of Duke Bernard. In Bohemia, the towns of Budweiss and Tabor were again garrisoned for the Emperor, and every precaution taken to oppose with energy the designs of the traitor.

As Gallas did not appear disposed to return, Piccolomini determined to put Wallenstein's credulity once more to the test. He begged to be sent to bring back Gallas, and Wallenstein suffered himself a second time to be overreached. This inconceivable blindness can only be accounted for as the result of his pride, which never retracted the opinion it had once formed of any person, and would not acknowledge, even to itself, the possibility of being deceived. He conveyed Count Piccolomini in his own carriage to Lintz, where the latter immediately followed the example of Gallas, and even went a step farther. He had promised the duke to return. He did so, but it was at the head of an army, intending to surprise the duke in Pilsen. Another army under General Suys hastened to Prague, to secure that capital in its allegiance, and to defend it against the rebels. Gallas, at the same time, announced himself to the different imperial armies as the commander-in-chief, from whom they were henceforth to receive orders. Placards were circulated through all the imperial camps, denouncing the duke and his four confidants, and absolving the soldiers from all obedience to him.

The example which had been set at Lintz, was universally followed; imprecations were showered on the traitor, and he was forsaken by all the armies. At last, when even Piccolomini returned no more, the mist fell from Wallenstein's eyes, and in consternation he awoke from his dream. Yet his faith in the truth of astrology, and in the fidelity of the army was unshaken. Immediately after the intelligence of Piccolomini's defection, he issued orders, that in future no commands were to be obeyed, which did not proceed directly from himself, or from Terzky, or Illo. He prepared, in all haste, to advance upon Prague, where he intended to throw off the mask, and openly to declare against the Emperor. All the troops were to assemble before that city, and from thence to pour down with rapidity upon Austria. Duke Bernard, who had joined the conspiracy, was to support the operations of the duke, with the Swedish troops, and to effect a diversion upon the Danube.

Terzky was already upon his march towards Prague; and nothing, but the want of horses, prevented the duke from following him with the regiments who still adhered faithfully to him. But when, with the most anxious expectation, he awaited the intelligence from Prague, he suddenly received information of the loss of that town, the defection of his generals, the desertion of his troops, the discovery of his whole plot, and the rapid advance of Piccolomini, who was sworn to his destruction. Suddenly and fearfully had all his projects been ruined—all his hopes annihilated. He stood alone, abandoned by all to whom he had been a benefactor, betrayed by all on whom he had depended. But it is under such circumstances that great minds reveal themselves. Though deceived in all his expectations, he refused to abandon one of his designs; he despaired of nothing, so long as life remained. The time was now come, when he absolutely required that assistance, which he had so often solicited from the Swedes and the Saxons, and when all doubts of the sincerity of his purposes must be dispelled. And now, when Oxenstiern and Arnheim were convinced of the sincerity of his intentions, and were aware of his necessities, they no longer hesitated to embrace the favourable opportunity, and to offer him their protection. On the part of Saxony, the Duke Francis Albert of Saxe Lauenberg was to join him with 4,000 men; and Duke Bernard, and the Palatine Christian of Birkenfeld, with 6,000 from Sweden, all chosen troops.

Wallenstein left Pilsen, with Terzky's regiment, and the few who either were, or pretended to be, faithful to him, and hastened to Egra, on the frontiers of the kingdom, in order to be near the Upper Palatinate, and to facilitate his junction with Duke Bernard. He was not yet informed of the decree by which he was proclaimed a public enemy and traitor; this thunder-stroke awaited him at Egra. He still reckoned on the army, which General Schafgotsch was preparing for him in Silesia, and flattered himself with the hope that many even of those who had forsaken him, would return with the first dawning of success. Even during his flight to Egra (so little humility had he learned from melancholy experience) he was still occupied with the colossal scheme of dethroning the Emperor. It was under these circumstances, that one of his suite asked leave to offer him his advice. "Under the Emperor," said he, "your highness is certain of being a great and respected noble; with the enemy, you are at best but a precarious king. It is unwise to risk certainty for uncertainty. The enemy will avail themselves of your personal influence, while the opportunity lasts; but you will ever be regarded with suspicion, and they will always be fearful lest you should treat them as you have done the Emperor. Return, then, to your allegiance, while there is yet time."—"And how is that to be done?" said Wallenstein, interrupting him: "You have 40,000 men-at-arms," rejoined he, (meaning ducats, which were stamped with the figure of an armed man,) "take them with you, and go straight to the Imperial Court; then declare that the steps you have hitherto taken were merely designed to test the fidelity of the Emperor's servants, and of distinguishing the loyal from the doubtful; and since most have shown a disposition to revolt, say you are come to warn his Imperial Majesty against those dangerous men. Thus you will make those appear as traitors, who are labouring to represent you as a false villain. At the Imperial Court, a man is sure to be welcome with 40,000 ducats, and Friedland will be again as he was at the first."— "The advice is good," said Wallenstein, after a pause, "but let the devil trust to it."

While the duke, in his retirement in Egra, was energetically pushing his negociations with the enemy, consulting the stars, and indulging in new hopes, the dagger which was to put an end to his existence was unsheathed almost under his very eyes. The imperial decree which proclaimed him an outlaw, had not failed of its effect; and an avenging Nemesis ordained that the ungrateful should fall beneath the blow of ingratitude. Among his officers, Wallenstein had particularly distinguished one Leslie, an Irishman, and had made his fortune.

> [Schiller is mistaken as to this point. Leslie was a Scotchman, and Buttler an Irishman and a papist. He died a general in the Emperor's service, and founded, at Prague, a convent of Irish Franciscans which still exists.—Ed.]

This was the man who now felt himself called on to execute the sentence against him, and to earn the price of blood. No sooner had he reached Egra, in the suite of the duke, than he disclosed to the commandant of the town, Colonel Buttler, and to Lieutenant-

Colonel Gordon, two Protestant Scotchmen, the treasonable designs of the duke, which the latter had imprudently enough communicated to him during the journey. In these two individuals, he had found men capable of a determined resolution. They were now called on to choose between treason and duty, between their legitimate sovereign and a fugitive abandoned rebel; and though the latter was their common benefactor, the choice could not remain for a moment doubtful. They were solemnly pledged to the allegiance of the Emperor, and this duty required them to take the most rapid measures against the public enemy. The opportunity was favourable; his evil genius seemed to have delivered him into the hands of vengeance. But not to encroach on the province of justice, they resolved to deliver up their victim alive; and they parted with the bold resolve to take their general prisoner. This dark plot was buried in the deepest silence; and Wallenstein, far from suspecting his impending ruin, flattered himself that in the garrison of Egra he possessed his bravest and most faithful champions.

At this time, he became acquainted with the Imperial proclamations containing his sentence, and which had been published in all the camps. He now became aware of the full extent of the danger which encompassed him, the utter impossibility of retracing his steps, his fearfully forlorn condition, and the absolute necessity of at once trusting himself to the faith and honour of the Emperor's enemies. To Leslie he poured forth all the anguish of his wounded spirit, and the vehemence of his agitation extracted from him his last remaining secret. He disclosed to this officer his intention to deliver up Egra and Ellenbogen, the passes of the kingdom, to the Palatine of Birkenfeld, and at the same time, informed him of the near approach of Duke Bernard, of whose arrival he hoped to receive tidings that very night. These disclosures, which Leslie immediately communicated to the conspirators, made them change their original plan. The urgency of the danger admitted not of half measures. Egra might in a moment be in the enemy's hands, and a sudden revolution set their prisoner at liberty. To anticipate this mischance, they resolved to assassinate him and his associates the following night.

In order to execute this design with less noise, it was arranged that the fearful deed should be perpetrated at an entertainment which Colonel Buttler should give in the Castle of Egra. All the guests, except Wallenstein, made their appearance, who being in too great anxiety of mind to enjoy company excused himself. With regard to him, therefore, their plan must be again changed; but they resolved to execute their design against the others. The three Colonels, Illo, Terzky, and William Kinsky, came in with careless confidence, and with them Captain Neumann, an officer of ability, whose advice Terzky sought in every intricate affair. Previous to their arrival, trusty soldiers of the garrison, to whom the plot had been communicated, were admitted into the Castle, all the avenues leading from it guarded, and six of Buttler's dragoons concealed in an apartment close to the banqueting-room, who, on a concerted signal, were to rush in and kill the traitors. Without suspecting the danger that hung over them, the guests gaily abandoned themselves to the pleasures of the table, and Wallenstein's health was drunk in full bumpers, not as a servant of the Emperor, but as a sovereign prince. The wine opened their hearts, and Illo, with exultation, boasted that in three days an army would arrive, such as Wallenstein had never before been at the head of. "Yes," cried Neumann, "and then he hopes to bathe his hands in Austrian blood." During this conversation, the dessert was brought in, and Leslie gave the concerted signal to raise the drawbridges, while he himself received the keys of the gates. In an instant, the hall was filled with armed men, who, with the unexpected greeting of "Long live Ferdinand!" placed themselves behind the chairs of the marked guests. Surprised, and with a presentiment of their fate, they sprang from the table. Kinsky and Terzky were killed upon the spot, and before they could put themselves upon their guard. Neumann, during the confusion in the hall, escaped into the court, where, however, he was instantly recognised and cut down. Illo alone had the presence of mind to defend himself. He placed his back against a window, from whence he poured the bitterest reproaches upon Gordon, and challenged him to fight him fairly and honourably. After a gallant resistance, in which he slew two of his assailants, he fell to the ground overpowered by numbers, and pierced with ten wounds. The deed was no sooner accomplished, than Leslie hastened into the town to prevent a tumult. The sentinels at the castle gate, seeing him running and out of breath, and believing he belonged to the rebels, fired their muskets after him, but without effect. The firing, however, aroused the town-guard, and all Leslie's presence of mind was requisite to allay the tumult. He hastily detailed to them all the circumstances of Wallenstein's conspiracy, the measures which had been already taken to counteract it, the fate of the four rebels, as well as that which awaited their chief. Finding the troops well disposed, he exacted from them a new oath of fidelity to the Emperor, and to live and die for the good cause. A hundred of Buttler's dragoons were sent from the Castle into the town to patrol the streets, to overawe the partisans of the Duke, and to prevent tumult. All the gates of Egra were at the same time seized, and every avenue to Wallenstein's residence, which adjoined the market-place, guarded by a numerous and trusty body of troops, sufficient to prevent either his escape or his receiving any assistance from without.

But before they proceeded finally to execute the deed, a long conference was held among the conspirators in the Castle, whether they should kill him, or content themselves with making him prisoner. Besprinkled as they were with the blood, and deliberating almost over the very corpses of his murdered associates, even these furious men yet shuddered at the horror of taking away so illustrious a life. They saw before their mind's eye him their leader in battle, in the days of his good fortune, surrounded by his victorious army, clothed with all the pomp of military greatness, and long-accustomed awe again seized their minds. But this transitory emotion was soon effaced by the thought of the immediate danger. They remembered the hints which Neumann and Illo had thrown out at table, the near approach of a formidable army of Swedes and Saxons, and they clearly saw that the death of the traitor was their only chance of safety. They adhered, therefore, to their first resolution, and Captain Deveroux, an Irishman, who had already been retained for the murderous purpose, received decisive orders to act.

While these three officers were thus deciding upon his fate in the castle of Egra, Wallenstein was occupied in reading the stars with Seni. "The danger is not yet over," said the astrologer with prophetic spirit. "IT IS," replied the Duke, who would give the law even to heaven. "But," he continued with equally prophetic spirit, "that thou friend Seni thyself shall soon be thrown into prison, that also is written in the stars." The astrologer had taken his leave, and Wallenstein had retired to bed, when Captain Deveroux appeared before his residence with six halberdiers, and was immediately admitted by the guard, who were accustomed to see him visit the general at all hours. A page who met him upon the stairs, and attempted to raise an alarm, was run through the body with a pike. In the anti-chamber, the assassins met a servant, who had just come out of the sleeping-room of his master, and had taken with him the key. Putting his finger upon his mouth, the terrified domestic made a sign to them to make no noise, as the Duke was asleep. "Friend," cried Deveroux, "it is time to awake him;" and with these words he rushed against the door, which was also bolted from within, and burst it open.

Wallenstein had been roused from his first sleep, by the report of a musket which had accidentally gone off, and had sprung to the window to call the guard. At the same moment, he heard, from the adjoining building, the shrieks of the Countesses Terzky and Kinsky, who had just learnt the violent fate of their husbands. Ere he had time to reflect on these terrible events, Deveroux, with the other murderers, was in his chamber. The Duke was in his shirt, as he had leaped out of bed, and leaning on a table near the window. "Art thou the villain," cried Deveroux to him, "who intends to deliver up the Emperor's troops to the enemy, and to tear the crown from the head of his Majesty? Now thou must die!" He paused for a few moments, as if expecting an answer; but scorn and astonishment kept Wallenstein silent. Throwing his arms wide open, he received in his breast, the deadly blow of the halberds, and without uttering a groan, fell weltering in his blood.

The next day, an express arrived from the Duke of Lauenburg, announcing his approach. The messenger was secured, and another in Wallenstein's livery despatched to the Duke, to decoy him into Egra. The stratagem succeeded, and Francis Albert fell into the hands of the enemy. Duke Bernard of Weimar, who was on his march towards Egra, was nearly sharing the same fate. Fortunately, he heard of Wallenstein's death in time to save himself by a retreat. Ferdinand shed a tear over the fate of his general, and ordered three thousand masses to be said for his soul at Vienna; but, at the same time, he did not forget to reward his assassins with gold chains, chamberlains' keys, dignities, and estates.

Thus did Wallenstein, at the age of fifty, terminate his active and extraordinary life. To ambition, he owed both his greatness and his ruin; with all his failings, he possessed great and admirable qualities, and had he kept himself within due bounds, he would have lived and died without an equal. The virtues of the ruler and of the hero, prudence, justice, firmness, and courage, are strikingly prominent features in his character; but he wanted the gentler virtues of the man, which adorn the hero, and make the ruler beloved. Terror was the talisman with which he worked; extreme in his punishments as in his rewards, he knew how to keep alive the zeal of his followers, while no general of ancient or modern times could boast of being obeyed with equal alacrity. Submission to his will was more prized by him than bravery; for, if the soldiers work by the latter, it is on the former that the general depends. He continually kept up the obedience of his troops by capricious orders, and profusely rewarded the readiness to obey even in trifles; because he looked rather to the act itself, than its object. He once issued a decree, with the penalty of death on disobedience, that none but red sashes should be worn in the army. A captain of horse no sooner heard the order, than pulling off his gold-embroidered sash, he trampled it under foot; Wallenstein, on being informed of the circumstance, promoted him on the spot to the rank of Colonel. His comprehensive glance was always directed to the whole, and in all his apparent caprice, he steadily kept in view some general scope or bearing. The robberies committed by the soldiers in a friendly country, had led to the severest orders against marauders; and all who should be caught thieving, were threatened with the halter. Wallenstein himself having met a straggler in the open country upon the field, commanded him to be seized without trial, as a transgressor of the law, and in his usual voice of thunder, exclaimed, "Hang the fellow," against which no opposition ever availed. The soldier pleaded and proved his innocence, but the irrevocable sentence had gone forth. "Hang then innocent," cried the inexorable Wallenstein, "the guilty will have then more reason to tremble." Preparations were already making to execute the sentence, when the soldier, who gave himself up for lost, formed the desperate resolution of not dying without revenge. He fell furiously upon his judge, but was overpowered by numbers, and disarmed before he could fulfil his design. "Now let him go," said the Duke, "it will excite sufficient terror."

His munificence was supported by an immense income, which was estimated at three millions of florins yearly, without reckoning the enormous sums which he raised under the name of contributions. His liberality and clearness of understanding, raised him above the religious prejudices of his age; and the Jesuits never forgave him for having seen through their system, and for regarding the pope as nothing more than a bishop of Rome.

But as no one ever yet came to a fortunate end who quarrelled with the Church, Wallenstein also must augment the number of its victims. Through the intrigues of monks, he lost at Ratisbon the command of the army, and at Egra his life; by the same arts, perhaps, he lost what was of more consequence, his honourable name and good repute with posterity.

For in justice it must be admitted, that the pens which have traced the history of this extraordinary man are not untinged with partiality, and that the treachery of the duke, and his designs upon the throne of Bohemia, rest not so much upon proven facts, as upon probable conjecture. No documents have yet been brought to light, which disclose with historical certainty the secret motives of his conduct; and among all his public and well attested actions, there is, perhaps, not one which could not have had an innocent end. Many of his most obnoxious measures proved nothing but the earnest wish he entertained for peace; most of the others are explained and justified by the well-founded distrust he entertained of the Emperor, and the excusable wish of maintaining his own importance. It is true, that his conduct towards the Elector of Bavaria looks too like an unworthy revenge, and the dictates of an implacable spirit; but still, none of his actions perhaps warrant us in holding his treason to be proved. If necessity and despair at last forced him to deserve the sentence which had been pronounced against him while innocent, still this, if true, will not justify that sentence. Thus Wallenstein fell, not because he was a rebel, but he became a rebel because he fell. Unfortunate in life that he made a victorious party his enemy, and still more unfortunate in death, that the same party survived him and wrote his history.